The U.S. Navy in World War II

PETER BENOIT

Children's Press®
An Imprint of Scholastic Inc.
New York Toronto London Auckland Sydney
Mexico City New Delhi Hong Kong
Danbury, Connecticut

Content Consultant
James Marten, PhD
Professor and Chair, History Department
Marquette University, Milwaukee, Wisconsin

Library of Congress Cataloging-in-Publication Data
Benoit, Peter, 1955–
The U.S. Navy in World War II / by Peter Benoit.
    pages cm. — (A true book)
  Includes bibliographical references and index.
  ISBN 978-0-531-20497-9 (library binding : alkaline paper) — ISBN 978-0-531-21732-0 (paper-
back : alkaline paper)
1. World War, 1939–1945—Naval operations, American—Juvenile literature. 2. United States.
Navy—History—World War, 1939–1945—Juvenile literature. 3. United States. Navy—History—
Juvenile literature. I. Title.
  D773.B46 2014
  940.54'5973—dc23   2014003936

All rights reserved. Published in 2015 by Children's Press, an imprint of Scholastic Inc.
Printed in the United States of America 113
SCHOLASTIC, CHILDREN'S PRESS, A TRUE BOOK™, and associated logos are trademarks and/or
registered trademarks of Scholastic Inc.

1 2 3 4 5 6 7 8 9 10 R 24 23 22 21 20 19 18 17 16 15

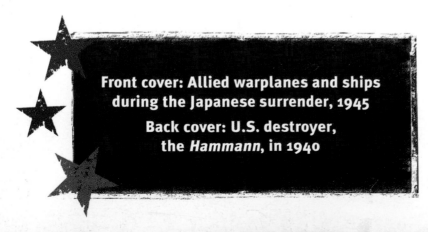

Front cover: Allied warplanes and ships
during the Japanese surrender, 1945

Back cover: U.S. destroyer,
the *Hammann*, in 1940

Find the Truth!

Everything you are about to read is true *except* for one of the sentences on this page.

Which one is **TRUE**?

The U.S. Navy's youngest sailor during World War II was 12 years old.

Japan formally surrendered on a Japanese warship.

Find the answers in this book.

Contents

THE **BIG** TRUTH!

The Ugly Duckling

U.S. Navy Shore Patrol

4

Marines and a hospital corpsman move a wounded soldier.

3 Fighting the War

4 New Horizons

Women made up about
2 percent of the U.S. Navy
during World War II.

Adolf Hitler meets with Japanese representatives in 1936.

CHAPTER 1

Going to War

War had been brewing in Europe and Asia long before the United States entered the fighting. Japan invaded Manchuria in 1931. For the next decade, Japanese troops worked their way south and west. In 1939, Germany invaded Poland under the orders of German leader Adolf Hitler. This sparked war in Europe. U.S. ships sent aid to Britain, the Soviet Union, and other countries. However, America officially remained outside the war. That changed on December 7, 1941.

Adolf Hitler's nephew served in the U.S. Navy during World War II.

Under Attack

Early on the morning of December 7, Japan attacked the U.S. Naval **fleet** at Pearl Harbor in Hawaii. Japanese bomber planes had taken off from six aircraft carriers cruising north of the U.S. base. The attack damaged 21 U.S. ships. Two of them were beyond repair: the USS *Arizona* and the USS *Oklahoma*. Hundreds of aircraft were also damaged. More than 2,400 Americans were killed. About 2,000 of them were members of the navy.

Sailors stand among damaged planes, watching as the warship *Shaw* (background, center) explodes.

The U.S. government created posters encouraging people to join the navy and other branches of the military.

Into the War

The United States declared war on Japan the next day. It declared war on Germany and Italy, Japan's allies, three days later. Men flocked to **enlist**. On the day of the attack, the navy included about 340,000 people. By the end of the month, that number had grown by nearly 42,000. By the end of the war, more than 4 million people had served in the navy. Most volunteered, though about 1.5 million were **drafted**.

Enlistment in the military skyrocketed following the attack on Pearl Harbor.

Young Men

The U.S. military—including the navy—required men to be at least 18 years old to enlist. Sometimes, younger boys lied about their age so they could join. They faked birth certificates or parents' signatures. Calvin Graham was one example. In 1942, he saved many lives during the Battle of Guadalcanal in the Pacific Ocean. Graham was considered a hero. He was just 12 years old.

Sailors Prepare for War

Men needed training to go from being **civilians** to being sailors. New **recruits** were given uniforms, underclothes, socks, shoes, bedding, and other items when they arrived for basic training. They were also given a canvas seabag. This bag would hold everything they owned. Sailors packed their belongings according to strict navy rules. This made sure everything fit in the bag. Rolling uniforms in tight bundles helped keep them free of wrinkles.

Men began to be drafted into the army in 1940. The navy started drafting in 1942.

New recruits practice laying out the contents of their seabags.

Before the war, basic training lasted 16 weeks. It was later shortened to four weeks, and then increased to six weeks. No matter how long recruits spent in training, it was intense. Officers barked orders at them day and night. Sailors learned to march, fight, speak, and act like navy men. They learned how to scrub a boat and how to take orders.

A group of navy recruits stands at attention.

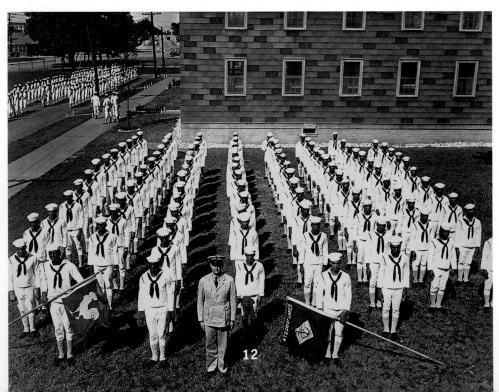

An American navy technician tracks Japanese ships on a radar chart.

After learning the basics, some navy recruits were sent directly into action. They learned their particular duties through active experience. Others stayed for additional training for certain jobs. They might learn to operate **sonar** or radar, which helped find and track enemy ships and planes. Some recruits studied medicine. Others learned how to fly navy aircraft. Some jobs required more training than others.

Navy men wore special coats and other items to keep them warm in cold climates.

CHAPTER 2

In the Navy

Once they entered the war, recruits settled in on ships or at bases. Life could be a little different depending on where a sailor served. In the Atlantic Ocean, sailors often faced cold weather and German submarines called U-boats. In the Pacific Ocean, they dealt with heat and Japanese aircraft. A sailor might be one of thousands on a battleship or be one of 12 crew members on a Patrol **Torpedo** (PT) boat.

 Submarine crews made up about 2 percent of U.S. Navy personnel.

Shipshape

No matter where they were, sailors on a ship had to keep it in top shape. Seamen scrubbed the deck, cleaned the guns, and kept the ship's interior tidy. Sailors often had lockers to store their possessions. Non-officers slept in metal and canvas beds called racks. These were set up in stacked bunks. Some officers shared rooms called cabins with each other. An important officer, such as the ship's captain, had his own private cabin.

Sailors rest in their bunks.

Men at a cruiser's snack bar, called a gedunk.

Chowing Down

People in the navy were fairly well fed. Cooks worked in kitchens called galleys. Food, called chow, had to survive being stored for long periods of time on the ship. Common dishes included chipped beef, bean soup, powdered eggs, and fried Spam. Spam was canned ham. On Christmas or Thanksgiving, the cook might produce a turkey for dinner. Many boats also had a gedunk, or snack bar. Gedunks served soda, candy, and, with luck, ice cream.

Men line up to dish food onto their plates as they sail toward the Pacific island of Iwo Jima.

Usually, sailors ate from steel trays and china bowls in the mess hall. Officers ate in a separate dining area called a wardroom. Certain duties required a sailor to stay at his post. In these cases, he ate wherever he was stationed. The meal was usually a simple sandwich and coffee. Coffee was by far the most common drink on a ship. Sailors called it joe. Another favorite of sailors was ketchup, which was nicknamed red lead.

Food shortages became a serious problem during World War II. Troops and civilians in war-torn areas suffered. Foods such as fresh meat became difficult to get. To help, U.S. Navy and civilian ships brought food to countries such as Great Britain and the Soviet Union. Spam was a big part of these shipments. It was inexpensive and easy to store, unlike fresh meat. Some 485,000 tons of canned meat were shipped to the Soviet Union alone.

Keeping Clean

Fresh water was limited on a ship in the middle of a saltwater ocean. A bath would be wasteful. Instead, sailors used a careful shower method. First they wet themselves down, and then turned the water off and covered themselves with soap. Then they turned the water back on to rinse off. Some sailors in the Pacific found another method. In a rainstorm, they simply grabbed a bar of soap and stepped out on the deck.

Water had to be used as efficiently as possible, even when doing laundry.

A sailor's white canvas hat has been called a Dixie cup, squid lid, dog dish, and many other nicknames.

These sailors wear the navy's classic white cotton uniforms.

A Sailor's Uniform

Some sailors wore the well-known blue wool or white cotton uniforms. The warmer wool was more common in colder weather. Cotton was lighter and better suited to higher temperatures. The pants in both uniforms were bell-bottomed. Other sailors wore blue jeans and a blue, button-up shirt. Officers and **aviators** generally wore khakis. These clothes were meant to be durable, surviving wear, tear, and many washings.

The Ugly Duckling

Throughout World War II, German U-boats sank huge numbers of both military and merchant ships. Every time a merchant ship sank, all of the supplies it carried were lost. Britain and its allies needed those supplies to keep the war going. With this in mind, the Liberty ship was created. In many ways, the food, weapons, tanks, troops, and other items Liberty ships carried around the world helped win the war.

British engineers originally designed Liberty ships. The ships were rough and simple. U.S. president Franklin Roosevelt nicknamed them ugly ducklings. But they were fast and easy to make. Engineers worked to speed shipbuilding. At first, a Liberty ship was built in 244 days. Later on, many factories were turning them out in an average of 42 days. Nearly 3,000 were produced before the end of the war.

Tailors were first established in the navy in 1869.

Fighting the War

Members of the navy could specialize in many different jobs. Gunners manned a ship's guns, while corpsmen gave medical care to crew members. Machinists maintained and repaired engines. Cooks fed the crew, and navigators mapped the ship's route. Signalmen communicated with other ships. Sonar and radar operators tracked enemy movements. There were also tailors, cobblers, barbers, and laundrymen. With sometimes thousands of men in a crew, a ship could be like a fully functioning town.

A corpsman provides treatment to a wounded marine at the island of Okinawa.

Corpsmen

Doctors, nurses, and assistants called hospital corpsmen provided medical care in the navy. Only hospital ships and large warships had room for doctors and nurses. Everywhere else, medical care was provided only by corpsmen. Some corpsmen were attached to marine units that fought on land. Navy corpsmen quickly earned a reputation for bravery. They often found themselves directly in the way of enemy fire while helping a wounded sailor or marine.

Security

The navy had to keep its bases, ships, and people secure. Sometimes, marines were used as guards. Sailors in the shore patrol watched over people who were in the brig, or jail. They also arrested or ticketed misbehaving sailors on leave. The navy had sailors on civilian merchant ships as well. These sailors were called Navy Armed Guards. They either helped the ship communicate or manned the guns that had been added to the ship.

Members of the shore patrol wore armbands with the initials *SP* to identify them.

Flying Over Seas

Being an aviator in the U.S. Naval Air Force was a challenge. Fighter and bomber pilots used the short runways on carriers for takeoffs and landings. **Catapults** launched planes into the air. To land, a hook caught the plane as it came in. This helped the plane stop before reaching the end of the runway. Pilots on other warships flew floatplanes, which could land on water. Floatplanes acted as extra eyes, searching for the enemy or for downed pilots in need of rescue.

Pilots climb onto a carrier's flight deck and walk toward their planes. Parachute harnesses are strapped to their backs.

A Landing Signals Officer's call sometimes meant life or death for a pilot.

On a carrier, aviators depended on the flight deck gang. They made sure planes took off and landed safely. The Carrier Air Group Commander (CAG) organized all of the takeoffs and landings. The Landing Signals Officer (LSO) waved colored paddles to signal to a pilot and help him land. If the landing did not seem safe, the LSO signaled the aviator to circle around and try again.

Special landing craft could come very close to shore to drop off troops during an amphibious assault.

Marines

Members of the U.S. Marine Corps were trained to fight on sea and on land. During World War II, they specialized in **amphibious** assaults. This generally meant arriving at an island or other territory by boat and swarming the beaches. The tactic was valuable in the fight in the Pacific against Japan. There, the marines used a method called island hopping. They pushed Japanese forces back toward Japan, island by island.

Paving the Way

Seabees often entered a territory after the marines and before anyone else. *Seabee* comes from the official name Construction Battalions, or CBs. They built new bases and expanded old ones. When U.S. and other troops invaded France in 1944, Seabees destroyed German-built barriers on the beaches. They then built a harbor so troops would have an easier time reaching the shore.

Seabees level the ground before constructing an airstrip for landing planes.

The Seabees were officially created in March 1942.

33

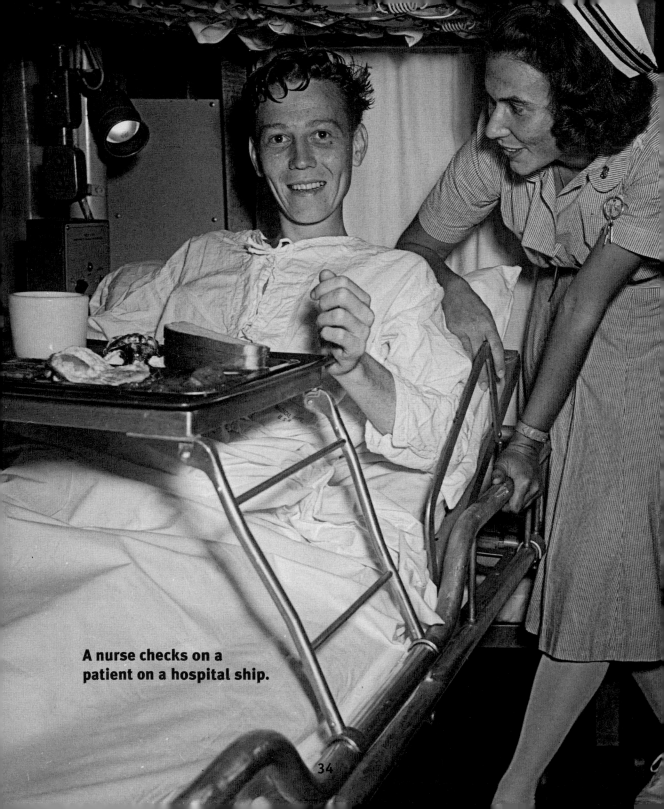

A nurse checks on a
patient on a hospital ship.

New Horizons

At the beginning of World War II, the U.S. Navy limited its opportunities to certain groups. With few exceptions, only white or Hispanic men were allowed to enlist. African Americans could enlist only as cooks or kitchen staff. Women could volunteer as nurses, but not for any other duty. In spite of the navy's limitations, members of these groups became heroes from the moment the United States was thrust into the war.

 The first U.S. hospital ship was used in the 19th century.

Beyond the Call of Duty

Seaman Doris "Dorie" Miller was an African American cook on the battleship *West Virginia* in 1941. The *West Virginia* was at Pearl Harbor when the Japanese attacked on December 7, 1941. Miller left behind his kitchen duties when the attack began. He helped load guns and fired one, though he had never been trained to. Miller also helped move wounded sailors to safety. He became a hero.

Doris Miller was the first African American to receive a Navy Cross, the navy's second-highest honor.

The Golden Thirteen were the navy's first African American officers, commissioned in February 1944.

First Lady Eleanor Roosevelt and organizations such as the National Association for the Advancement of Colored People (NAACP) spoke out for the inclusion of black men in the navy. Thanks to their support, more opportunities opened up for African Americans in this military branch. By 1944, some ships were manned largely by black sailors. That same year, the navy welcomed its first black officers, the Golden Thirteen.

WAVES recruits march in formation during training.

WAVES

World War II created a huge need for sailors. To keep up with the demand, the navy created a new unit for women volunteers in July 1942. The unit was named Women Accepted for Volunteer Emergency Service, or WAVES. The navy appointed the first female naval officer, Lieutenant Commander Mildred McAfee, to run the WAVES. WAVES took over navy jobs in the United States so that more men were freed to go into combat.

Thousands of women enlisted. By 1943, there were 27,000 WAVES. By the end of the war, nearly 100,000 WAVES and 8,000 WAVES officers were active. Several of them were African American, after the WAVES was opened to black women in 1944. Women served as part of the navy, coast guard, and the marines. Many of them worked as secretaries. Others repaired aircraft or sent coded messages. Some forecasted the weather or trained pilots and gunners.

A WAVES machinist starts the propeller of a navy plane.

Unbreakable Code

Codes kept the enemy from knowing what troops were planning or doing. The one American code the Japanese never broke was the marines' code. Starting in 1942, the marines used Native American speakers called code talkers to send messages. Most of them—about 420—were Navajo. Like many Native American languages, few people spoke Navajo. This meant that not many people were familiar with the language, making the code harder to break.

Timeline of the U.S. Navy During World War II

MARCH 1942
The Seabees are created.

DECEMBER 7, 1941
Japan attacks Pearl Harbor naval base.

The first 29 Navajo code talkers enlisted in the marines in May 1942. They created a dictionary of code words, replacing military terms with Navajo vocabulary. Each code talker memorized the dictionary before going into combat. During battles, code talkers sent and received messages about enemy movements, marine locations, and other information. They took part in every Pacific battle involving the marines from 1942 until the war ended. Many of these battles were won with their help.

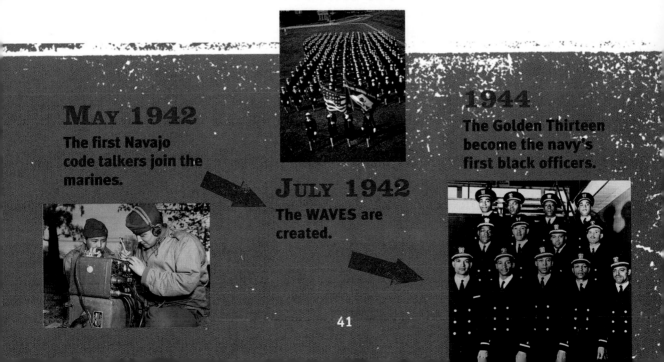

MAY 1942
The first Navajo code talkers join the marines.

JULY 1942
The WAVES are created.

1944
The Golden Thirteen become the navy's first black officers.

A Deadly End

The Allied armies, including the United States and Soviet Union, forced Germany to surrender in May 1945. But the war with Japan dragged on. When a bloody battle on the island of Okinawa ended in June with more than 12,000 American deaths and 150,000 Japanese deaths, U.S. officials were considering ways to end the war. U.S. president Harry Truman decided to use the new **atomic bomb**. The bomb destroyed the Japanese towns of Hiroshima and Nagasaki before Japan surrendered. ★

People walk through the destruction left in Hiroshima, Japan, a few months after the atomic bomb was dropped.

On the USS Missouri

Japan formally surrendered on September 2, 1945. The ceremony took place in Tokyo Bay on board the battleship USS *Missouri*. More than 250 other warships filled the rest of the bay. Representatives from Japan, the United States, China, Britain, the Soviet Union, Australia, Canada, France, the Netherlands, and New Zealand all signed the surrender agreement. The ceremony did not take long. After years of war, the signing of the document took less than half an hour.

Number of U.S. presidents who served in the navy during World War II before becoming president: 6: John Kennedy, Lyndon Johnson, Richard Nixon, Gerald Ford, Jimmy Carter, and George H. W. Bush

Number of amphibious ships in the U.S. Navy in December 1941: 0

Number of amphibious ships in the U.S. Navy in August 1945: 2,547

Number of ships in the U.S. Navy in December 1941: 790

Number of ships in the U.S. Navy in August 1945: 6,768

Number of U.S. sailors and marines killed, wounded, or missing during the Battle of Okinawa: Nearly 50,000

Number of people who served in the U.S. Navy during World War II: More than 4 million

Did you find the truth?

The U.S. Navy's youngest sailor during World War II was 12 years old.

Japan formally surrendered on a Japanese warship.

Resources

Books

Benoit, Peter. *The Attack on Pearl Harbor*. New York: Children's Press, 2013.

Stein, R. Conrad. *World War II*. New York: Children's Press, 2012.

Stein, R. Conrad. *World War II in the Pacific: From Pearl Harbor to Nagasaki*. Berkeley Heights, NJ: Enslow Publishers, 2011.

Visit this Scholastic Web site for more information on the U.S. Navy in World War II:
www.factsfornow.scholastic.com
Enter the keywords **U.S. Navy in World War II**

Important Words

amphibious (am-FIB-ee-uhs) — able to travel on land and in water

atomic bomb (uh-TAH-mik BAHM) — a very powerful bomb that explodes with great force, heat, and bright light

aviators (AY-vee-ay-turz) — people who fly aircraft

catapults (KAT-uh-pults) — devices used to launch airplanes from the deck of a ship

civilians (suh-VIL-yuhnz) — people who are not members of the armed forces

convoys (KAHN-voiz) — groups of vehicles or ships that travel together for convenience or safety

drafted (DRAFT-id) — required to serve in the armed forces

enlist (en-LIST) — to join or get someone to join the army, navy, or one of the other armed forces

fleet (FLEET) — a group of warships under one command

merchant (MUR-chuhnt) — a type of ship that carries goods for trade

recruits (ri-KROOTS) — people who have recently joined the armed forces or any group or organization

sonar (SOH-nahr) — an instrument used on ships and submarines that sends out underwater sound waves to determine the location of objects and the distance to the bottom

torpedo (tor-PEE-doh) — an underwater bomb shaped like a tube that explodes when it hits a target, such as a ship

Index

Page numbers in **bold** indicate illustrations

About the Author

Peter Benoit is the author of dozens of books for Children's Press. He has written about American history, ancient civilizations, ecosystems, and more. Peter is also a historical reenactor, occasional tutor, and poet. He is a graduate of Skidmore College, with a degree in mathematics. He lives in Greenwich, New York.